THE BLOOD OF MY HEART

RAHUL KUMAR

Copyright © Rahul Kumar
All Rights Reserved.

"This book is dedicated to everyone who suffers more in imagination than in reality."

Contents

Contents

Foreword

Poetry written with *heart connects with the heart*. The book *"THE BLOOD OF MY HEART"* is a collection of *original poems* by the writer. One by one the poems unfold the *experience of love* in the most amazing way. The book makes you smile with poems on *fresh, innocent, and young love*. It ignites those memories of intense love you had for someone. It fills your heart with sadness when the writer expresses hurt and pain in love. Then it makes you emotional with heartbreaking words about separation in love. The writer doesn't end the book with the sadness of love but shows the best of his craft by channelizing that pain into his life goals. You will not even realize how swiftly the book moves from love to life and how the writer's words become inspiring to move on in life. The writer's vocabulary and language command stand out and make it an *unforgettable* reading experience. The poems in the book are *heart-touching, heartwarming, intense, delicate, emotional, sensual, inspiring, motivating, and relatable*.

- Garima Soni, CA & Author of the book - 'Life Simplified'

Acknowledgements

I express my sincere gratitude and heartfelt thanks to all my readers, who gave me their valuable feedback on my debut novel - *'The Fig Flower'*, which encouraged and motivated me to continue with my endeavors in writing. My readers shall continue to be my biggest source of inspiration in my literary journey.

My parents and my two sisters have always been my biggest source of motivation. Though, I spent the last year away from them here in Delhi but never missed them as they make me feel at home on video calls every single day. I like my own company but I embrace their company more. I think this book could have been a lot better, more emotional, sensible, and immense.... if they had been with me during this last year.

My friends (close, best and special) have been very helpful in my literary adventures. Their wholehearted support has been instrumental in shaping the final version of this book. They have significantly contributed to the contents of this book, through active discussions on various topics deliberated in this book. I won't mention few names here from whom I got the experiences and very indispensible life lessons. They have invariably been the parts of my parallel and imaginative world. And now that world is shattered for me.

Aakash & Hitesh (Our Tripod) both of them have done an excellent job of proofreading the manuscript and enhancing its appeal significantly. I thank Notion Press for helping me throughout the publication process and helping me come up with such a beautiful and amazing gift for all my readers. Thanks Aayush for listening very composedly to all the crazy thoughts of my mind, everytime.

I would also like to give my heartiest thanks to all those fantastic people who have written beautiful and very apt lines in praise for this book. Their kind and lovely words instilled enthusiasm in me to bring this book before all of you. Abhishek Sir, Sanjeev Sir, Debotosh Sir and Debojyoti Sir, I can't express my heartfelt gratitude to all of you for such a kindness and encouraging words. I would love to mention a very special name, Garima Soni Mam for her very beautifully written forward for this book. Thankyou so much.

And last, but certainly not least, you, the readers. I hope your unconditional love for my book will be touching a new feat every day. Goddess Santoshi blesses all of you!

Finally, I thank God for his abundant blessings. I couldn't ask for more.

About The Book

"The Blood Of My Heart" is an eclectic melange of ethereal *Love, Life, Separation, Reflections, Disappointments, Suicidal Thoughts, Heartbreak, Struggle, Beauty, Beningness, or... dramatic & romantic* wishes that are waiting to be fulfilled. The first part of the book will provide you a sneak peek into *A Realm Of Love*, an author's parallel & imaginative World and the rest are an expression of his inner journey through life, experiences & beyond. The poems speak of a never-ending yearning for love & nostalgia on one hand and deriving inspiration from life on the other hand. These beautiful lines entail all shades of an individual i.e, a child, a son, a lover, an ardent who forgets to love himself. These are fluttering musings of early restless mornings & late awakened nights that form words, lines, and stanzas. These are the rises of *flurry* in a *disquiet heart* that want to be quietened or *thirst* in a sizzling love that wants to be quenched. These are the *palimpsest of memories* filled with different hues of love, & ever-changing shades of life. These are the *potpourri* of thoughts that spreads fragrance in their surroundings. These are the *flashes* in the eyes and *musings* of the mind. These are the *tears* that never got turned into drops yet witnessed crying one's heart out. *'Sensual, intense, insane, igniting, and utterly heartfelt.'*

Praise For The Book

"The book is full of *refreshing, exciting, mesmerizing,* and brilliantly crafted *romantic* poems and a lot more. *Evincive, sensual* and *sensible* writing from such a young capable writer augurs well for a promising and laudable future. Looking forward to reading more from this gifted writer. Overall, A *sensual, intense, fascinating, igniting,* and *utterly heartfelt piece.*"

- Abhishek Singh, *IAS & Actor*

"Sensuousness, romance, and love are the hallmarks of poetry. Feelings are well expressed through the words that help you to go deep into the romantic era of the literary world. It's a praiseworthy effort as those sensitive to humane feelings will enjoy reading it. Wishing Rahul the best of luck in his endeavors and wish him success always."

- Sanjeev Shekhar, *HR Professional & An author of two bestseller*

"Rahul's poems speak for themselves. With simple diction, they are *crisp* and *enchanting,* besides being laced with *sensible* messages. Readers would surely enjoy the book."

- Debotosh Chaterjee, *IRS & an author of the bestselling Book - '8 Things To Do When You Turn 20.'*

"*Love* is depicted in vivid hues, where *joys* and *sorrows* are synonymous in these powerful expressions from the true life experiences of every individual by this young poet in this book. The readers will truly feel relatable and close to their heart the power of love and its pain and happiness which I, as a reader truly felt. I really fall in love with his *honest* expressions of love in words. I must appreciate his work and I'm sure everyone will love his mesmerizing web of words which will leave everyone spellbound. Waiting to read more by this young poet in the future.''

- **Debjyoti Das Rana,** *a poet & a published author of the book - 'Only For You, My Love'*

My Experiments With Love

' Beauty with no humility is no beauty. "

1. What is love?

Love is the first sight flurry
In the heart,
And the last sight wanting desires.
It's an exchange of beautiful gifts,
Wearing each other's smiles,
It's a sharing of hot spicy Maggie
In the late winter afternoon
With the same spoon,
It's wiping the stains of oil
Strewn on each other's faces.

Love is taking
100s of photos together,
Not posting a single one of them ever
As these are the memories
Which remains forever.
Love is searching for the heart
Which pulsates yours
In a room crowded with people
Feeling your heart flutter
When their eyes lock with yours.
Love is letting them
Have all the freedom
Even though, you have confined
Yourself to them
And they are the last resort
Of yours,
Love is meaning it every time
When you say,
'You're mine
And I'm all yours.
Love is stealing gazes,
When you are sitting with them,
Love is talking to them
Straight for hours on calls
When you both are far away
From each other.
Love is calling them to see

How they're doing
At least once a day.
Love is respecting them
When you're in an argument.
Love is embracing them
Even if you have nothing to say.
Love is the happiness
In their presence,
Love is the calmness
In their absence.
Love is never having any doubt
In their love for you,
Love is knowing that
No matter what goes wrong,
You will find your person
Always by your side.
Love is being certain that
They will never make you feel
Less of a person.

2. A Love Or A Habit

Restlessness has crept up
On my mind,
Strongly feels like
The clock of the heart
Is getting rewind.
Feelings of being hugged
All the time,
The wire connecting
Our hearts
Endlessly chimes.

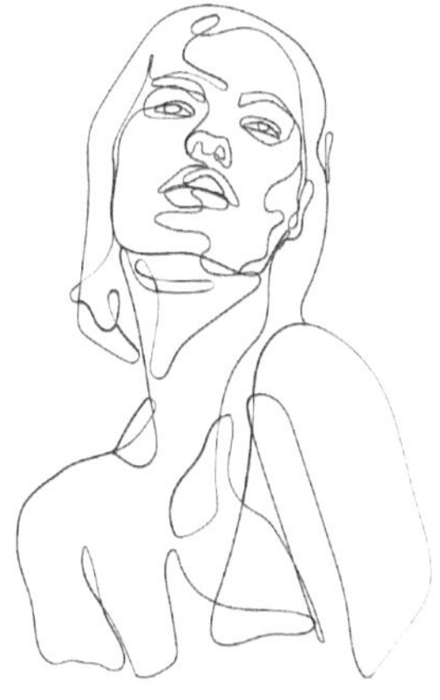

Fear of separation
Before even coming
Close to you
Stopping me to express
My infinite love to you.
Can't stop myself now
Developed the sheer habit
Of consoling myself
Every time,
When I strongly feel like
Drowning myself
Into the ocean
Of your love.

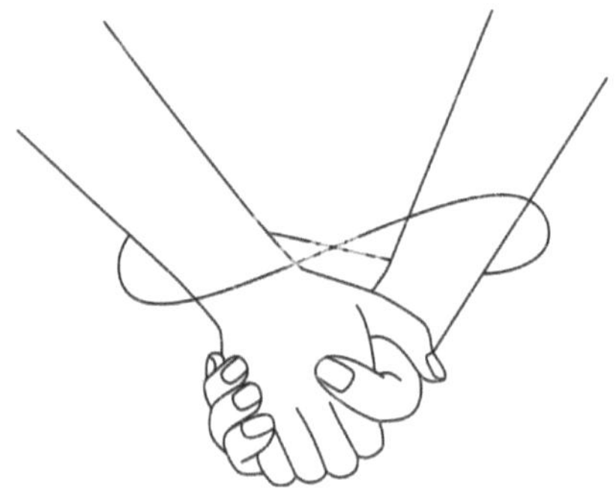

Never let any confusion
Block out the door
Which connects the yard
Of your heart,
To the grounds of my soul.
Keep reminding myself
All day & all night
That you complete me
To reach my ultimate goals.

Shower of your love,
Respect and care,
Douses all the evils
Approaching me.
Living always in dread
As if this fountain will soon
Come to an end.
Never meant that
You're only mine
But want to tell you
For a long
That I'm only yours.

Never knew,
How love is defined,
You are my love
Or my habit
Little I knew.
Dead sure,
It's not a habit
As try every day
Even completed
The 21 days full circle
To give up this habit
But closing my eyes
Welled with tears,
Every night
Without

The slightest regret.

Heart defines love,
Beats differently
Inside everyone.
Talked, walked,
And laughed,
Felt every touch,
Mind in a sheer endeavor
To find that rythm
Inside her
Which matches with mine.

My ideals, principles,
& EVERY SINGLE THING,
Are Ready to deceive
As many times as possible.
Need your hint,
Just Once.

3. Love Or Shy

Love or shy,
Never get her actually,
After so many tries.
Such a caring soul,
Promises me,
She never ever lies
TO ME.

On her scale of care,
Love and attention,
Having the highest position

Myself I find.
Don't know why
More often in despair,
I cry.

If I share that promises
With someone else,
Having countless complaints,
On her lips
And Putting her finger
On me
Says, you lie.
Only one confusing thing
About her,
Neither let me go

Nor pull me to her side.

Tired of new hopes
With each passing day,
Just addressed
With an instant bye
For this only,
Go to college
Every single day.

Her coming to me
Arises an explicable
Curiosity & excitement.
Ensconcing beside me
In the class,
Leaves me shy
As if a butterfly
In my stomach
Flies.

Insecurities or understanding?
Bringing her friend along
On EVERY DATE
Whenever she arranges,
Having excuses on fingertips
Oiled my hair or so
Every time WHEN I CALL
Increases my challenge.

Isn't it unfounded?
Better say,
It's her desipience,
Her feeling unsafe
And to have even
The slightest misgiving
On the one & only
Who born only
To make her feel safe.

To take you
To the land of stars,
To save you
From the ready-to-devour evils.
Nothing can be more disheartening,
It's you and
Your considering me
As if the Avatar of the devil.

Conveying love through
Touches, holding hands,
Putting the head
On the shoulder,
Hugging all day in & day out,
Ain't my thing perhaps.
It's no less saddening
Your understanding
ABOUT LOVE
Stops here
As I'm all yours
And here only
To save you
From all mishaps.

4. My Darlingtest

Though break high into my breath
Like a reek heaves up vertically
In a still halcyon wind;
Disheveled hairs billowing all the time
Frolicsome mood bearing lively & playful body
Like a reek-drift in a light wind.

Mere sole touch feels me
Like a wind felt on the face
In a slight Breeze,
Goosebumps like leaves rustle,
Vanes moved by the wind;
Another touch whirls me in
Like leaves & twigs
In constant motion,
In a gentle breeze.

Thy holding my hand
Raises dust, Looses wrappers,
Stirs in me the desires
Like small branches shifts
In a tender breeze;
Thy egging on me to feel
The same what thou feel
Leaves the leaves to sway;
Like crested wavelets
Form on inland water
In a fresh breeze.

Extant daydream
On the edge of being waned
Like large Branches in motion,
Walking inconvenienced,
Whistling heard in telegraph wires,
Almost destroyed,
In a sturdy breeze.

5. Striving Heart

Just a mere glance of hers
Tig the wire of my heart.
Coming to me always
With a long intact smile
Incenses the fire inside
A little, I know
What, how, who I am?
When sitting with her beside.

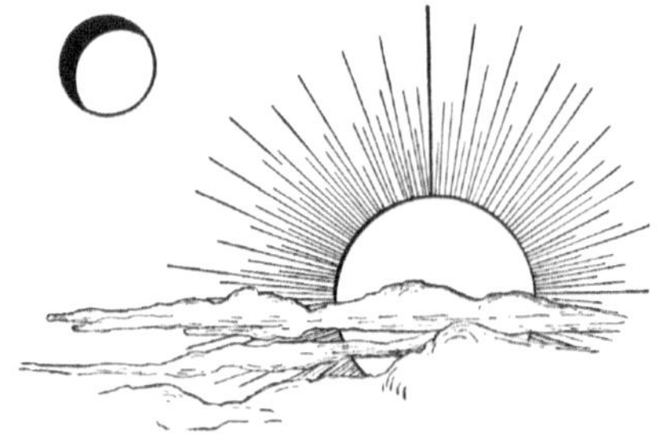

Have started forgetting
My sorry past
Since I met her.
Tears roll down my cheeks still
Of happiness,
And brightness now
The meaning of life
Has also started changing
Just because of
The intensity of love
For her, inside.

Feel like seize this moment sometimes
Inside the four sides of the wall of my heart
To never come out.

Strongly feel like making peace
With the tears, & killer thoughts
That has been disturbing me
For ages,
All day and night,
Inside and out.

6. Love Triumphs

What is this blissfulness
To the depth of the ocean,
Where sunset looks like a wonder,
To the heights of the clouds
Where the ground misses the rain,
To the length between the stars,
Where they shine distance apart.
To those lengths, heights, and depths
You are my limitless magical wonder.

Unlike those eight wonders,
Love is no certified wonder.
But once a touch of love,
Forever the eyes stay without a blink.
For always, the feet stay unmarred,
And you, my darling, for me,
Is the soul to lean on.

The cry in the grief,
The loudness in the laughter,
The conspiracy of time.
The compensation of destiny.
Love frowns for never,
At last! It triumphs like ever.

Oh! The world of billions
Accuse me, if I am wrong
Instil me, you are no wrong.
Declare love as a discomfort
Say love is destruction.
And I would say,
You have never really loved.

7. Paradise Lost

Without a glance
Of your face,
My morning doesn't start.
Until your fragrance melts
Into my breath.
My heartbeat seems to be lost
Somewhere.
My heart is secure
In your arms,
Your smile is everywhere.

Just look into my eyes,
There's a house of yours somewhere.
You are my only darling
My beginning as well as my end.

I'm drowning
And lost in your eyes,
All day and all night.

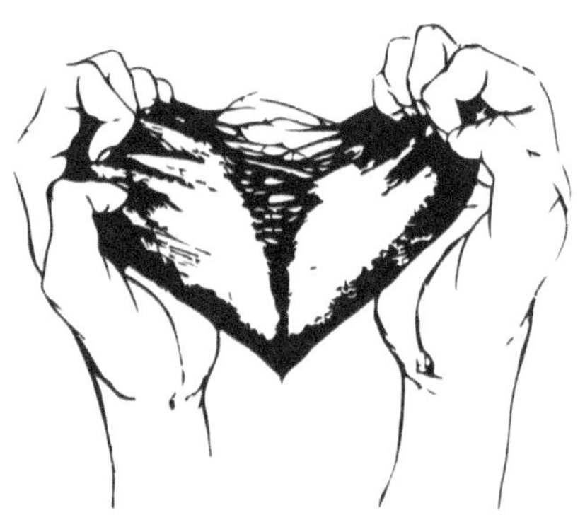

Prayers don't work for me now,
Medicines don't work anymore
Since my heart has fallen for you
My sleeping in the nights
My love in the conversations
My peace, you've cheated them all.
When I take a deep breath
When I close my eyes
I only see you, my beloved,
This has happened to me
For the first time.

The winds keep asking for you
And I'm tired of telling them
Why do the stars talk to me about you
Now your stories are on my lips
I accept my love for you,
My beloved.

8. Realm Of Love

There's no going back
Either your love will make
Or it will destroy.
Just want to hear a lie;
That was wrong
And this is right.
Please let those words
Come out
Which you are hiding
On your lips.

I'm yours & you are mine.
Your breaths are always
Attached to mine.
Please say those three magical words
Give me relief from this trouble,
Once and for all.

Completely overwhelmed by the intoxication of love,
Feet don't rest on the ground anymore,
Flying in the sky of love,
Only endless springs and fountains of love,
Everywhere I found.
Have taken a step into the realm of love, now.
There's no going back from here,
Your beautiful eyes gazing at me,
Killing me bit by bit.

This sweet poison of love,
I am going to keep drinking.
You may not be God
But I will continue to pray,
And bow to you.
The dreams have no place
In my eyes,
As they are already flooded
With tears.
You may not love me,
Accept my love for you
At least.
Have taken a vow to myself now
Either live with you
Or kill myself.

9. My Only Ardas

Wish I could express my heart.
Wish one day,
You may understand my feelings,
Pain inside given by your eyes,
No less deadly darts.
You are in my thoughts,
You are in my dreams
In my heart, 24/7
Left with no choices,
And places,

RAHUL KUMAR

Where shall I go?
My heart is flooded
With the stream of your love.
Banks are devastated,
Now, where shall I stand?

Seems Implausible to live
If you're not around.
Only wish to be around you.
Wish to live with you
Or die without you.
My love for you
Is inexplicable & boundless,
Never wanted more,
Or less than you.
You're my heart,

you're my life
You are my everything.

In the street of your heart,
My heart is lost somewhere
Had you been with me,
My life would have been a lot better.
My life is now yours,
what do I do?
You've got to believe me.

RAHUL KUMAR

Will wait for you in this life
As well as in the next.
Wish I could express my heart to you,
My inexplicable & infinite love for you.

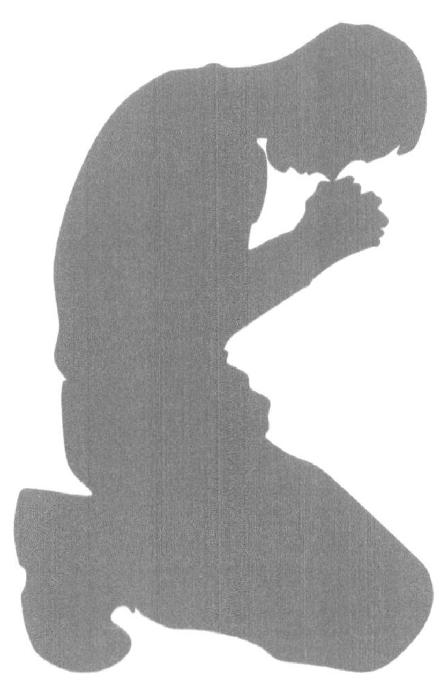

After leaving you,
I am dead.
You're my shadow,
In your face only
I see my God.

My wish, Oh,
is that I bow to you always,
Carol your name
All day & all night.
You are in my every wish,
My Ardas (PRAYER) to my God.

10. What Kind Of Love Is This

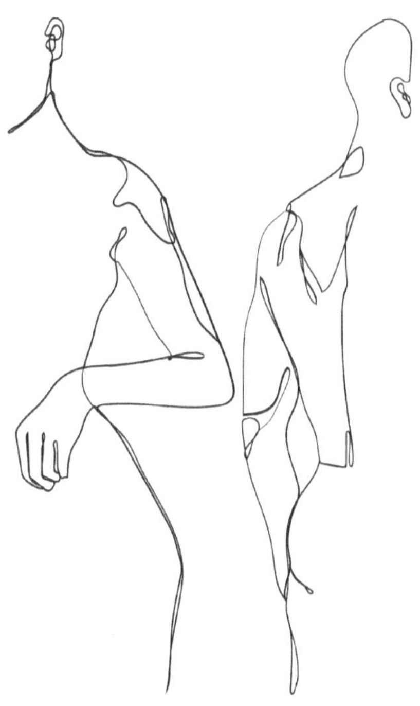

If I have to live without you,
Then what kind of life is this!
If I can't console myself,
Then what kind of lover I am!
There are cries of two separated hearts
Everywhere,
If I can't pass the fire test of separation
Then what kind of love is this!

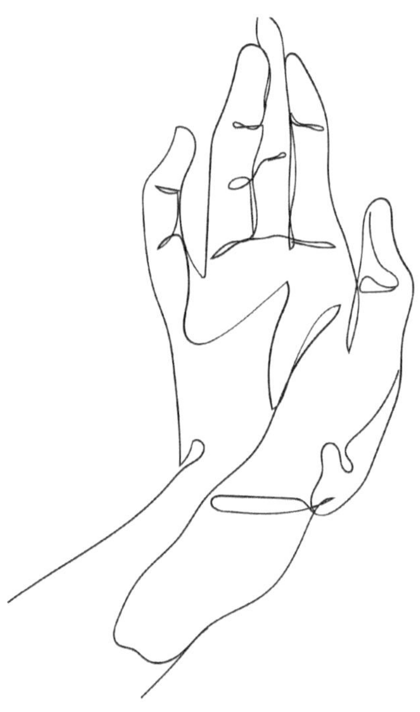

Your fragrance is strewn everywhere,

Your lines are in the palm of my hands,
Don't know why you are not in my fate!
This innocent heart is searching for you
Everywhere, the proximity to you.
How God can be so unmoved,
Watching the destruction in the silence
Of the two lovers in love.
It's impossible to forget you.

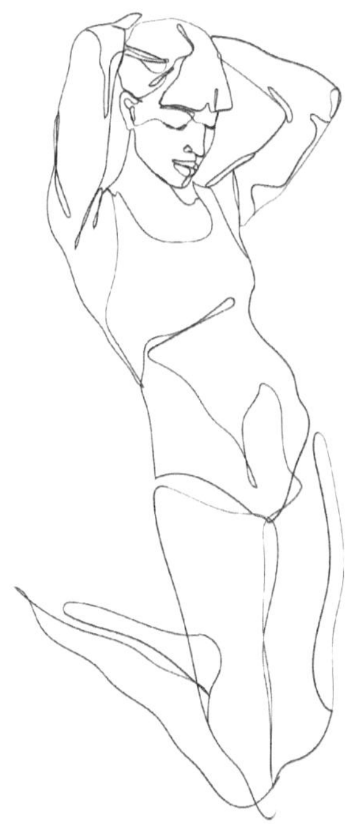

11. Fire

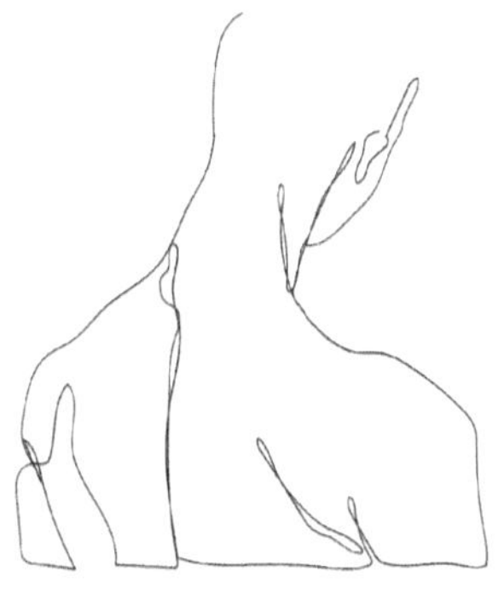

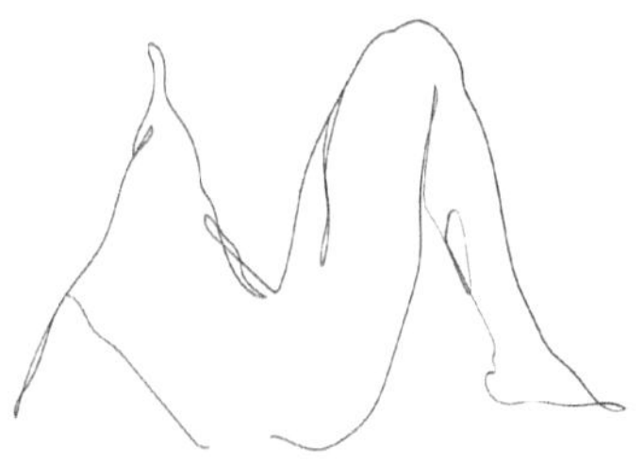

Wish I could get you earlier,
A fire burning inside,
Wish we burnt together.
Have I come complete

After meeting you
Or was I better alone?
You are my strength
Or becoming my weakness?
Passing every moment counting,
As if repaying some debt.
Days are passing in restlessness
Nights are awakened.
This torture is devastating
Pain of separation is unbearable
Because of you only
Has it been possible,
That I live again.

Heaps of small dreams,

In which there are songs,
In songs, there is life,
love, and longing.
Stopped dreaming those,
In which you aren't there.
Opening these lips, look
that I had kept closed yet.
My heart believes you so much
As I don't even believe in myself.
In my lone moments,
I dream about you,
I have fallen in love with you.

12. Please Come

What should I do to my legs,
No matter how much I resist,
They find their way to your heart.
What should I do to my hands,
No matter what picture I draw,
They end up with your image.
The winds have started whispering in my ears,
Bees have started buzzing too,
It is only me who is crazy
In love with you,

Or you are crazy too.

Your absence troubles my heart,
All the time,
Even I don't know,
Why you are necessary for me?
My sleep never returns
Once they left,
So many nights have passed,
In counting countless stars.
So much so,
My fingers are burned.

Why you lied to me?
Why you betrayed me?
What compelled you
To kill my belief?
Why you didn't even hesitate
To do this sin?
Those eyes whom I,
Used to adore so much,
Without any reason,

RAHUL KUMAR

In those very insidious eyes,
Why there is no love left for me?

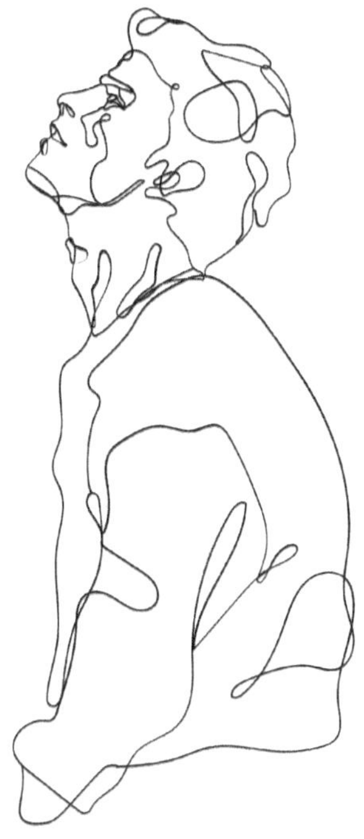

Alive or dead?
I can't tell.
Have lost my heart
Somewhere,
In search of the same,
Last day,
Came across sorrow

On the way,
I hugged & wept,
That heart was mine,
Only mine,
Why did I lose it?
I can't understand.
You are my last hope,
You are my last breath,
I don't have my heart anymore,
How can I give it
To someone else?
Never share my love,
With others,
I keep loving only you.
Even if you are not there
In my life.
Why are you taking my test,
Please come to me
From somwhere,
It's difficult,
To live without you.

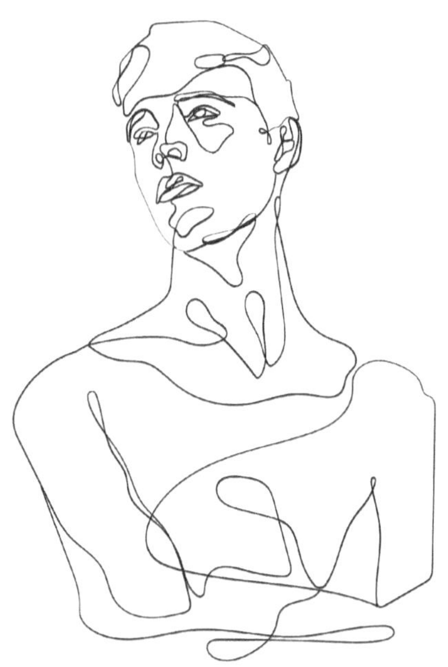

13. Reminders Of Her

I didn't forget,
Those days full of colors,
Smile intact on my face,
I still remember those nights,

Which always fell short
Before our singing together
Those songs of love.

Sending me your pictures
Wrongfully wrapped yourself in saree
Asking me how you looked
Whether the same is properly hooked?
Your frowning at me in all innocence
When I burst out laughing.

Me knocking at your door for the first time
Remember?
Your mommy's endless inquisitions to me
Where did I come from & who the hell I am?
Remember?
Your advancing towards me
And your panicking
Your eyes pleading to me
Grabbing the notes from my hand

RAHUL KUMAR

Driving me away without inviting.

Your coming close to me the next day
Made me frightened
A slap was expected
How the hell did I commit that impertinence?
To my surprise, you started crying
Down your beautiful cheeks
Those precious pearls endlessly rolling
Your hands and lips trying

To say something but continuously failing.

You were never gonna stop
Until me keeping those pearls safe in my hanky
Remember?
Caressing, patting & appeasing nothing worked
Unless me taking you in my arms and holding you strongly
You were so stubborn not stopping
Finally worked,
Whispering something in your ears.

Remember?
Those words made you giggle at once.

As luck would have it
Our coming together was mere a chance
Remember?
Your going away from me gradually
Giving in to distances & circumstances
It was not an excuse anymore
Your separation from me

It was all our preordained destiny.
I'm dead sure
You haven't forgotten me still
Since we are separated.

God's separating us apart brings no good
As we continue having glimpses,
Previously in the school, now you continuing Your schooling, me
going for coaching there
Upon crossing & facing me

RAHUL KUMAR

Remember?
Your smiling while climbing the stairs.
Left with no other choices
Never getting the second chances
Me surviving those difficult days with mere those glimpses.

In this race of life,
In such a way, situations unfolding
Imprinting you in my memories forever
I continuing my journey further

Your forgetting me or not never bother.
But you surely don't remember
How it became difficult forgetting
Counting stars in your memory
Those days my fingers burning.

Today, while passing through the market
I met your shadow which you left behind
Even after reminding it many a time
Those memories floating in my mind

Your face still flashing in my eyes.
It's been seven years
Such a long time without you
Since we last met
You would have forgotten me
Possibly, my love is not over yet.
But treated like a stranger.
Again failed touching.

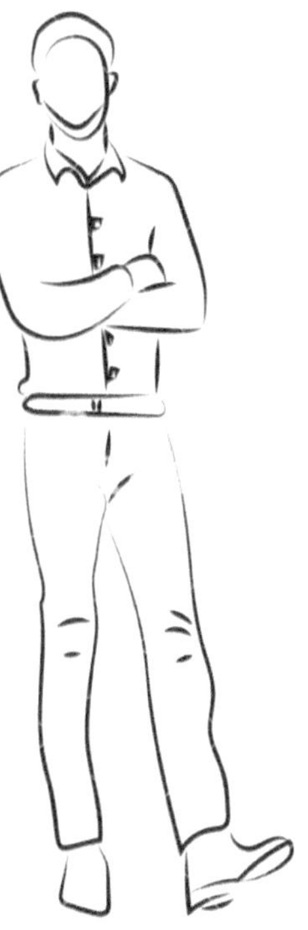

14. Love Is Caged

I believed
In your idea of love
Since we first met.
You love birds,
Great.
Put one in a cage,
Have it iterate,
Whatever you say,
Give it food,
Nurture it,

And above all,
To never let it fly away,
Keep the cage fastened,
Not even if it wants to.
Wow, this is how love works!
I keep believing,
I grow up thinking.
Love is caged,
Or it isn't loved at all.

Have lived so far
In your confinement,
How can now freedom
Means to me anything?
Such fear in my heart,
It lingers on

Under my skin too.

Despite all these sufferings,
To find the same
Old love again,
In my life,
I still hope to meet you.

15. Love Is Mine

I never moved on,
Not from you,
Not from my sorry past,
The ones I loved before.
The love I gave,
Remains safe
In my heart,
All of it,
It keeps me warm

THE BLOOD OF MY HEART

On a dull winter morning
As I sit & think of you,
Not pain but only nostalgia
I am filled right now.

More often feel
A flurry in my heart,
Something like hope,
Like faith, something good,
That's worth keeping.
I know it sounds,
Just all about myself,
Not you or the others,
But that is what
It has become now
This love,

It has become mine
Just mine.

16. The Blood Of My Heart

Had lost faith,
In the aroma of love.

Where she came from,
A little I know.
Clouded me,
Spreading her fragrance,
Belying my conjectures,
She made me believe,
Love again is possible.

Broke promises,
Which I made

A long back to myself,
In the fire of love,
Will never put my hands.
Where would I go?
Afterall
With inflamed heart,
Once again.

Love at first sight,
She tells

Is no less delusion.
Her moving her hands
For friendship,
Her coming close to me,
Gradually,
Now her hands on my neck,
Throttling that belief,
Once and for all,
Completely.

Seeking comfort,
Shameless,
Tired, & helpless,
My heart
Falls &
Stuck in her lap,
In her scarf
Which she swaddle
Caressing,
Patting it like a baby
She makes my heart
Rest & sleep in her lap.
For my heart too
Never wants to awake
From its never-ending slumber.

So great of her,
She too didn't try
To wake it up.
Surrounded by aroma,
In her bodily warmth,
My heart went in coma.
Didn't want to see,
Me getting slow death,
How innocent,

How caring,
How sweet of her,
Stabbing the knife
Into my heart,
Even a bit,
She didn't stumble.

Strewn on her scarf,
Her hands smeared,
The head is Red,
Splashes on her face,
Everywhere,
Body too soaked up with
The blood of my heart.
Her hands shaking,

Her body failing,
How will she wipe it,
Where will she hide it?
The perverse color
Of my blood,
Indelibly haunting,
Even in next birth seven,
It's not gonna leaving
For my heart,
Your lap is heaven.
Only for you, my love
My heart is destined for beating.

17. Why?

*Why did they come
Into my life?
If they were destined
To be gone.
Why did they make
Every moment beautiful?
If they were finding
It hard to carry on.
In place of memories,
Which were supposed to be*

Beautiful and lasting,
They left behind
A lifelong-painful-
And-harrowing experiences.
Why they make
Themselves available?
When I was not
In their calender
Biological,
So, the casual too.
Why they faked
Everything?
If they were
Pretty sure about
Their inner voices.
Why they make
Me dream those things?
For them as they said
Which were not gonna
Practically possible.
Why they make
Me imagine of
A Parallel
And a peaceful World
Of me and them only?
When they always
Adored the company

Of nuisance
Around them.
Why they were dying
To be part
Of every reason
Of my happiness?
If they already
Made their mind
To let me suffer
On myself,
Whenever
I needed them
The most.
Why they made
Me reach
To a limitless sky?
If they were supposed
To be not there,
When I looked back
In consternation
And fear of
Loosing my grip
From the ladders.
What were those
Incessant touches,
And frequent gestures,
Pressing their bosom

Against my soldiers,
Making me believe
That I am
The one and only,
Eclectic well
Which holds the capacity
To quench their
Never-ending thirstiness.
What were those words?
Which felt me like joke
As they released smile
After every pause,
In actuality,
They meant those words,
Every single of them,
Which are now
Becoming the reason
Of my never-ending sadness.
Why did they make
Every meeting special?
Why did they sound
Contented and happy?
If all the things
Were not gonna
Make my win
In love
Possible.

An understanding soul
What I think of them
From the day first
Then what made them
Finishes in one go
That they are confused,
When it comes to me,
And my promises.
Why they were
So dishonest
With me,
And themselves too,
All those times
When I was only
And only honest
And open to hear
Them, about them,
And what they
Think about me
In return,
Only I got blamed
For all those things
Which they said
In one go,
This is only
The product
Of my imagination.

Why they gave me
This lifetime punishment?
For the crimes
In which
Only they were involved
From the very outset.
In actuality,
The only mistake
Which I have done is
I didn't do any
Such thing
With them.

18. A Black Hole

What did I do wrong?
They broke that promise,
Which we made
To each other.
Leaving me alone,
Desolated, terrified,
Disappointed, & broken.

Had wishes for them only,
When raised my hands in prayer.
Taken a vow to be theirs only,
Until & after death too.
What will it take,
To expect the same from them?
Shall I bleed to death,
To prove my love for them,
The minimum one can do,
Maximum I will kill for them.

Hardly left any stone unturned.
Camouflaging or inherited,
How one can be so loving,
How one can be so caring,
Beyond my understanding,
How can they be disgusting,
At the same time.
Never knew them
Even after a million tries.

Fear creeps up,
Would never come out.
When I try,
Diving deep into their mind,
No less a black hole
That allures me,
Many a time.
A charming personality,
Or a clever mind?
The way to their heart,
No less a meander,
Hardly one triumph,
Risk is high
Of losing oneself

In search of the same.

My condition resembles fearful Karna,
In sheer consternation and agape,
Unable to unleash his protective guard,
Standing helpless and disappointed,
Having lost all his knowledge
On the battlefield before the opponent.

19. Leaving Is Painful

Their decency

To understand

Our care, attention

And infinite love

For them,

As mere a silent lifeless toy

Which could be changed,

Upon boredom.

It's hard

To let them go,

That is what,
We understand.
Their momentary care
For us,
Beguiling love
Toward us
Making us believe
In their every word
At times,
We become so used to
Having them with us
Most of the time,
All the time,
The idea of them
Not being there, anymore,
Doesn't sit well with us.
It's not that hard.
It's us
Who choose not
To go away from them,
Taking all the pain
On us,
Turning our eyes
Away from reality,
Just holding on to
In all those instances,
When they were not bad

For us.
Using their best
Of the times with us,
As immediate excuses,
We move ahead
To self-destruction
By compromising
With the pain,
Which they caused
To us.
In consternation,
We embrace
The fear of separation,
Which crept upon us,
Leaving them
Would cause us pain,
Ignoring the fact
That having them
Will do more harm
Than better.
Sometimes,
We let them
Break us as
They complete us.
Holding on to
The darkness,
We continue

To search for light,
Holding on to
The pain
We continue
To search for happiness,
Which doesn't make sense,
At all.

20. A Wish

Wish! a flower would fall
On this barren heartland.
Wish! a rain would quench
The thirst which resides,
Inside.
Wish! a bird would chirp,
Bringing the same,
Back to life.
Wish! the coming of someone

Would sweep
These rattling solitude
From this barren land.
Wish! someone would settle
This disquietened dust
With the splashes
Of her wet hair.
Wish! the same would find
A benevolent caretaker,
One day,
Who would embrace
This barrenness,
And would say & do,
'I'll put you first,
And nothing else matters'
Kind of love.
Wish! a soft eye would turn
Towards this silent street,
Inside
Wish! a first step
Toward the same
Would banish
All the indifferences
Of ages.
Wish! a chuckling
Would resonate
This desolated heart.

Wish! the dribbling honey
From those lips
Would pump the blood
Inside
Bringing the same,
Back to beat
With agility & vigor
For so long,
It has strived.
Wish! this barrenness
Would believe,
And would have
The same trust
On the impending rain,
As before.
Wish! there would be no place
For the hurt, the anxiety,
And the confusion
Inside,
Which those infidelities
Brought to life.
Wish! it would feel like
Trusting the process
Blindly, once again.
Wish! someone would
Enter this life,
At the most unexpected time.

Wish! it would belie
All those self-cocoon
Fear of confusion,
And mistrust.
Wish! despite telling myself
I won't let love
In again,
I would welcome the same.
With open arms
Realizing its thrust.
Wish! a burst of infectious laughter
Would delve
Into this counting-it's-days life
Wish! the same would bring
The kind of sunlight,
One could never resort
To mislay.
Wish! a heart would tangle
With mine,
And everything would finally
Fall into place.

21. Things Which Made Me Survive

Remember the years
That rolled by
Before you meet
That one heart.
The experiences,
You had
And the friends,
You made.

Whenever it feels
Difficult to move on
From the same heart,
Remember the way
The moon always
Made you feel
More comfortable
And shone a little bright too
& there was always a fragrance
In the ambiance,
Which smeared you
With delight,
And how life always
Made you feel
Soft & light.
Remember,
That blind stranger
The one whom,
You made cross the road,
Also those hands
On your head,
Which unconditionally
Rose in blessings.
Remember,
Those stories
Which brought tears
In your eyes

Of happiness,
Of sorrow
Which invariably inspired,
And made you survive.
Remember,
The moments,
You had,
The late nights,
When the books
Became your best friend
With whom you laughed,
And cried your heart out.
All those days,
Which you spent
in that horrible darkness,
In hope
For the new brightness.
Remember,
Those very moments
Which made you learn
To move on
From that first
Stupid heartbreak.
Remember,
When you told yourself,
'This time it feels so real,
But you got back up, again.

Remember,
How your heart
Learned to heal.
Remember,
The smiles,
The laughter,
And the tears
That drained your eyes.
Remember,
How you continued
To live,
And to learn,
And you did not realize,
How life beautifully
Passed by.
Remember,
The years that flowed,
Effortlessly
Before you met
This person.
Remember,
Every experience,
You had,
The hurt,
And the happiness,
And how much
You had to give.

Never ever have
This thought, that
Life will never
Be the same, again.
Remember,
How you experienced life,
Graciously
Before that heart
Mazed with yours,
And, even if they leave,
You will learn to live.

22. A Maze Of Desires

I like mornings,

I love sunsets,

The company of dark night,

Stars hanging,

Reminiscent of love.

Of happiness.

Of hope.

No less adore moonlight,

And late-night-walks

With you
Which feels divine.
I believe in you,
And your holding my hand,
Carrying my shopping bags,
On our weekend plans.
Putting your hands
On my shoulder
And in 'how are you',
& in your 'sweet dreams' messages.
No less adore
Those soft words
Which always dribble
From your lips
Touches my heart
Like infinite kisses.
Sometimes, It feels like,
I'm in a never-ending slumber,
Brushing your thumb
Over my hand
Makes me lumber.
A gesture so small,
And so unnoticed.
Yet, it has the power
To topple my world
From 'not okay' to 'I'm okay'
In an instant.

I believe in tomorrow.
Hopeful tomorrows.
Saver tomorrows.
Tomorrow that carries you
In my dreams.
And makes me believe
Yesterday doesn't matter,
Anymore.
Tomorrow that is destined
To be lived with you.
I believe in forever,
Not the kind that lasts
But the kind we always
Stay together.
The kind of forever
That witnesses
Shaking of your hands
And failing of your lips,
When you even have
The slightest thought of
Going away from me,
That swells your eyes
With tears
And your heart
With nostalgia.
Forever that remains
As unspoken words

And promises laced
Between them.
Forever that holds
Two hearts intact,
Saving the same
From destruction.
Forever that makes me feel
Your presence,
Even when you
Are not there
To hold my tears.
When solitude
Creeps upon my mind
Then plead to me
To spare this innocent body,
Those kinds of forever.

My Experiments With Life

"Love remains the same, it just changes the body."

23. Happy Birthday To Me

First seven years in lampblack smeared eyes,

Never learned how to make a tie.

Annoyed with my ringy hairs

Still remember my mom

Forcefully making ponytails

Me collecting the fallen hairs

On the ground

With tears welled in my eyes,

The mind filled with happiness

For cotton candy after getting it sold.

A five rupees coin in my fist
Before going to school every day,
Buying all the happiness in it,
Except for new clothes,
Waiting for the arrival
Of my next birthday.
Unable to hold my pant well
Till I reached puberty
In hands
Got the hands of my sis
A big responsibility
Still carrying well.
Me, my heart, and my ears all deployed
& Awakened throughout that long dramatic night,
For welcoming a new fairy
After a long, continued shrieking cry
Who made our world bright.
Years kept passing
Naughtiness would never end
Little does I know
How many times
Ended up
Hands tied with ropes
By every birthday ends.

Buddha getting enlightenment
Under the Bodhi tree
Company of my teachers
Sets me free
From laziness to the curse
Which sets my area apart
As a graveyard of dreams.

Breaking the vicious circle for me
Was never been easy
Still trying till the last breath
Every time
To do it bit by bit.

Always made the knowledge my strength
Never thought of earning money as my end
Still stuck in this vicious circle
My fellow friends
Won't take my last breath until & unless
Freeing their world from this ominous and gradual end.

Once again wishing
A happy birthday to me
With this end.

24. A Turning Point

How it feels
With dire situations
You deal.
Darkness all around,
Only disappointments
And troubles,
Each & every single time,
You find.

In those dire situations,
Days well-spent
In adjusting yourself.
In night,
A dreadful cloud surrounds.
A well of Death is right there
In front of you
Consciously your legs are in,
Helplessly, you find.

On that dreadful night,
Nothing in your hands,
Feels absolutely helpless
As if a dog hounds.
Only promises, expectations

And Condolences
By which you are bound.
Daydreams start petrifying
In the tension
Of a bleak future ahead
While dreams every night,
Start horrifying.

All day and night,
Only and only
An ominous voice
Sounds.
Until a night sets

RAHUL KUMAR

Carrying stars infinite,
Once in a blue moon,
Yourself you find.

The one and an only
Turning point,
Going back remains
Not an option, anymore,
Except sailing through
The extant tough streams
Just only for the sore,
Anyhow, you will have to find.

25. Systematic Sterilisations

Hopes, dreams, & desires
Carrying in our eyes
Leaving our home behind,
Since time immemorial,
To fight our destiny
Which miserably conspires.

After meeting the bitter reality
Of this dream world,
Nowhere to go
Tears welled in my eyes,
All the more,
Very difficult to hide.
Where education is a fashion
Depends on the moods
Of its proponents
Sometimes, in trend
And most of the time
In the anion.
Where there are left
No place for curiosity,

Hardly a day goes
Without
Suppression of budding voices
Suicidal thoughts, stress, depression &
Mental health crisis is all
Where shall we go now?
Left with such horrific choices.
Why shouldn't we call,
It's totally unfounded?
Where discussion goes on,
Straight for hours
On the conditions of oppressed,
And suppressed.
Isn't it ironic,
The proposer of the same
Never spent a minute
Out of his comfort zone,
AC room, & grandiose arrangements.
Among the best
Of the best higher institutions,
You pick one.
Hardly any single place
Is spared
From the curse
Inflicted upon
The so-called mother civilization
Of the world.

Where sleeping administration
Is shaken by just one minor protest.
And then the very next day
Coming of the statement
That they won't let
The temple of education
Become the hub of ideologies,
Presents a clear picture of
The systematic sterilization of education.

26. A Reminder

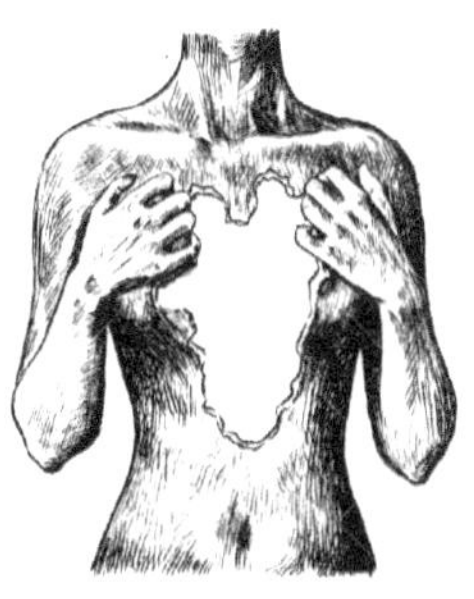

Taking a grim step
Of killing an innocent body,
A soul can't be at rest.
How can someone
Be so pathetic
Putting one's parent's
Upbringing
On fire test?

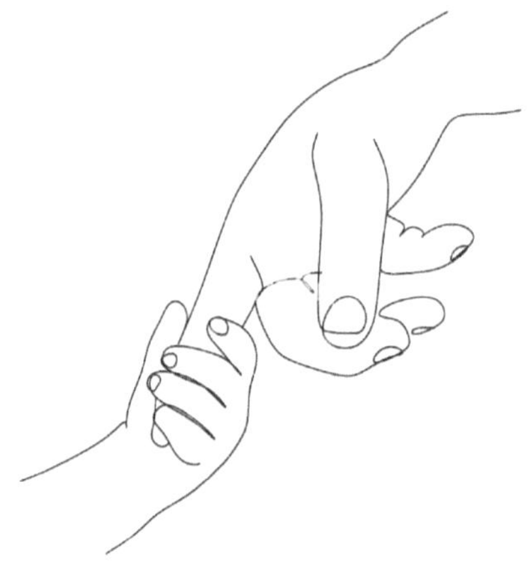

Walk barefoot,
Pass a whole rigorous year
In a single piece of cloth
While Buying toys, new dresses,
And sweets,
Never had the slightest hesitation.
The tiredness of the day
Never stopped them
To reject the wishes
Of their children
They can even walk
Up to hundreds of miles.

Sacrificing their entire life
Looking after their heir
Cremating the body of the same
The things which a father,
And a mother, exceptionally,
Never ever thinks of
While alive.

Those days full of struggles,
Sleeping empty stomach,
A firm pact with simmering troubles.
From the street foods,
Turning their glances
To save some coins if any
Turning us down
They never want
Putting the same
In our tiny little palm
Whenever,
We started crying.

For you only,
Faced all kinds of dire situations
Such petty suicidal thoughts
They never had
Unlike you, how shameless,
Sinistrous,
Better leave the thoughts,
They were finding it hard
So they tried
To take out their lives.

It's you
Who never grasped,
How hard they worked,
What tragedies they faced,
How they survived?
You are out
To kill that innocent life
Which they nurtured
On mere finding it hard.

27. Panchar Wala

From Rising before the sun

To Beat the sunset

Finishes his day

With a grandiose meal,

And contented mind,

In whatever he gets,

After such a long day.

Burns in the furnace

All-day,

And shudders in the winter

All night
Like the sun,
And the moon.
One does this
To brighten the world
With its light.
To unending destitution,
And mishaps,
The other gives a tough fight.

Rashes everywhere
On the body
Stains of dried sweating
As if the process of salt
In making.

RAHUL KUMAR

Even after liquidating his body
Throughout the day with water,
Ends up releasing
The same amount
By end of the day.

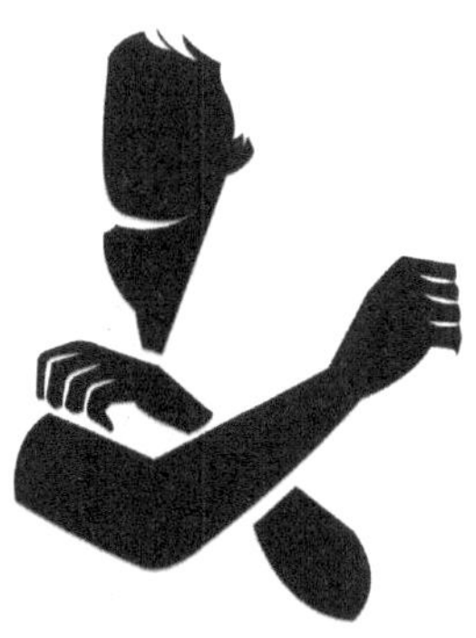

Small height, muscular body
Smeared with an odd smell
Black grease, dirt & dust
Everywhere,
Spending all day, no less,
In a rotting hell.

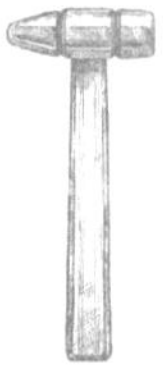

Always carrying minor injuries
On foot, thumb, and fingers,
Never stops his hammer
As he has a family to feed
Not a community to impress
For an only reason,
He is alive today
Never put his family to death
By hunger.

28. Pushing The Limits

In the never-ending race of life,
Little did I know
Its meaning ever,
Been directed
And pushed
Towards unachievable goals
Always,
Now learned to live
With this,
Forever.
Arrived at the stage,
Strongly feels like
Never looking back.
Afflictions deep

RAHUL KUMAR

Within my heart,
Mind and soul
Are far more extreme, now
Horrifying
And not letting rely
On my past.

Just a passenger of life
Start everything
With sheer excitement
Hardly ever feel tired,
At the very outset.
Tries to pass all the tests
Which life puts before
A feeling of me

Being a human too
Pulls me down,
And left me
with irreversible damages
To the body, soul,
And mind.
Throughout the horrific years
Of childhood,
Falling sick, severely,
Many a times
Was no less disastrous.
Born with preordained destiny
Written with the ink
Of blood, anger,
And afflictions,
In the period of the dark
Clouded night.
My body is not made
For the thickness,
Food eats me,
Liver is weak,
Grown-up
Hearing all this,
Every single time.
Gonna overcome
All these evils
Once get puberty

That sheer happiness is all
That made me survive.

As if a scapegoat destined
For being meals
For the crowd
After being cut down
Into several small pieces.
Left untouched,
Without a single scratch,
Seems like a divine interruption
In the meantime.
Right or wrong?
Feels sometimes,
Life is no less

A mimic
As it can't mean only
Pushing the limits.

29. A Middle Class Guy

Having a vanity
Of being the luckiest,
With hands
In an empty pocket.
Eyes revving
In an illusion,
Tears turn into mirrors,
Reflections of self,
Inside
Even the future

Can't create horror.
Doing away
With all needs,
Abandoning
All desires,
Becoming
Self-contented,
It's frivolous,
And unfounded
To talk of
A devout saint only
When it comes
To sacrificing oneself.
Crying one's heart out,
Pillow drenched in tears,
With not even
The slightest sound,
This is the minimum,
Everyone can do.
Stopping tears
Into a rolling drop,
Next to impossible,
For others
To hide pains, disappointments
And restlessness inside.

No safeguard against
Setbacks, afflictions,
And approaching death
Treated as a commodity
Until the last breath.
Even a genitor
Becomes calculative.
Why invest afterall
In such a vile,
Only born
For sucking blood
Bringing existing
To ruins
No less a sandstorm
Approaching and turning

Everything into dunes.
Immeasurable, & Implausible
To reach the bottom
Of his mind.
The top is as limitless
As infinite sky.
Bringing stars
To its knees,
Only he can do
Just need a hand
On his shoulder & head
And the rest will be history.

30. Misdemeanor

Millions of dreams,
These eyes carry
Unfulfilled, tamed,
And cowed.
Yearning youth helpless,
And hopeless,
Screaming for justice
For the crimes
Which they are unknown.
Washing dishes

With the ashes
Of their dreams
The lifelong trade-off
With afflictions
They are put to daily
Worn out of their fate
At times
Still left with
Resilience
Nonpareil courage
Of which they are
A lively example
Living in an inexplicable
Cloud of silence.
Chained invisible,
If it is for sound
Then their anklets
Which are put in their legs
Since childhood
Shaped and brought up
To not cross the sill
Otherwise,
Considered a misdemeanor.

31. A Debt

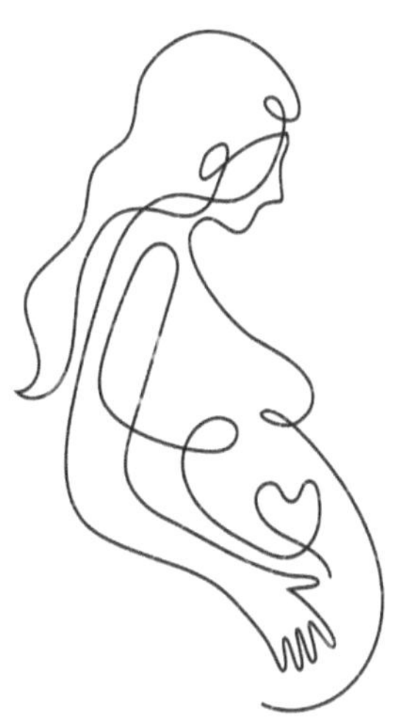

How will I
Pay your debt
Conceiving me
In your belly
For so long.
Taking every pain
On yourself
Saving me

From every evil
Putting kajal
On the forehead
And behind the ears.
Taking every bad word,
Spoken for me,
Fighting your husband
Standing always for me
Serving the food
Before me, first
Pressing my legs
Before my sleep
Having several doubts,
Do you even care
For yourself ever?
As you never
Leave me alone
On myself ever.
Awaken with me,
Sitting beside
On the bed
Sharing my every pain
The whole night
Only you can do,
Putting ointment
On my every wound,
Caressing the same

With neem leaves,
Moving in Panic
When I started
Screaming,
More you appeared
In agony
When I stopped eating.
Feeding me
With you hands always
Down your cheeks,
Tears endlessly rolling.
I was no less a devil
Who keeps you disturbing
Because I never wanted it
To be sharing
Such an attention seeker,
Greedy in your love
After, all the best efforts,
Stopped crying
Only
when you running
Towards me.

32. Move On

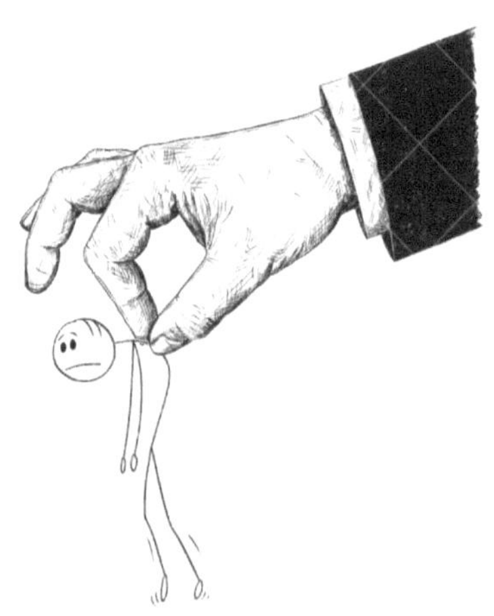

Whatever the situations,
You are in,
Try to move on.
Not only from stoppages,
From success as well.
It's not easy
To contain Success,
Don't hold on.
Why stagnate yourself?

Every day/every hour
Every moment
Try to improvise yourself.
You can make new learning,
Just need perspective.
Life throws away
New surprises,
Once we start
Moving.
Try to make it large.
In every relation,
The expectation is more,
The desire to move on
Towards it, is less.
The employer wishes
To pay more
To an employee,
Who goes the extra step,
Works towards the goal.
To work more avidly
The employee
Awaits the employer,
To pay more.
The intention is the same
On both the ends,
But none
Wanna risk their stake,

At the first end.
Whoever moves on
Awards is waiting
In line.
Be the first one
To walk the 1ˢᵗ step.
Holding on to
Achieve success
No less a failure,
In the long run.
Holding,
Onto your failure,
No less debt in crisis.
Failure equips us
With more tools,
Not to fail
In the same situation,
Same strategy,
And at the same level,
Again.

33. A Ray Of Hope

There's a ray of hope exudes
From every single thing
In this universe
Making me believe
In myself
Making me see
A thriving
And prospering future.
Despite my insecurities,
Despite my fears,
It makes me believe
It's what, I deserve.
Despite all the challenges that
I've failed to
Live up to
The dreams
That I've yet to fulfill.
This obstinate hope
Is the one
Instilling faith in me
What I can make happen &
What I can achieve.

There's no going back
Giving up is not an option,
Anymore.
Not now, not tomorrow,
Not ever,
Not because
Giving up is a sign of failure,
It's a sign
That I no longer hold
In heart of mine.
It's a sign that I don't see
Any point,
In getting up, once more.
It brings the prospect
Of a bright future,
Making me see
All my wishes
Coming true.
A love, friendship,
And a room filled
With people celebrating me.
A bright, dewy morning
With a sunrise
Brightens up my day
A mild evening
Where being alone
Doesn't make me feel,

Alone.
It's easy to get lost
In the months,
And years that pass me by,
Without realizing
Just how much
This life can do
For me, and
How much
I can do
For myself.

34. Upbringing

Born and brought up
In such a way,
Always carrying
My heart
On my sleeve
For anyone
Who shows
Even a little bit
Of kindness.
Forgiving too easily
And too quickly,
Always giving chances,
Once, twice, thrice
And even four
Even after getting hurt
Many a time.
My heart aches
Seeing someone enduring,
Even the slightest pain.
Without expecting
The same in return,
Love everyone,

Unquestionably,
Too much
And too deeply
Letting people break me
Taking me for granted
Many a time.
Am I too much soft?

35. Let Them Go

Such a difficult thing
To do,
Yet in our best interest
To let things go,
To take care of mental,
And our emotional health.
As it is no less deadly,
Looking at one
Who makes you
Incredibly happy

And also the reason
Behind your pain.
No matter how happy
They make us,
It's them
Who also cause
Undeniable strain.
Giving in remains
An only option,
Until & unless,
We can be happy
In their presence,
Once again.
They are meant
To stay
In our life
Till here only
If pain always follows
The happiness
That they bring.
Sometimes,
The most beautiful lessons
Are the hardest.
Sometimes,
Leaving is the most difficult
Out of the rest to do.
To love ourselves,

Letting them go
Who can't give us
The love,
We deserve
Is the most prudent
Thought,
We must serve.

36. Untitled

I used to be so much,
Now I'm nothing;
Buried beneath the grave
Of what used to be a flower.
Everlasting, yet forgettable,
Like one too many sunsets
Try to shake off the feeling
I get that my skeleton is no longer bones
But the dust settled for too long,

Hidden behind the pile
Of another's trophies and triumphs.
Looked at, but never seen;
It's like I picked my life
Out of a movie scene,
With too complex a plot,
In the script a useless dot,
How the hell do I even go on?
I used to be so much,
Now look at me;
Buried underneath the ground
As a constant state of mind.
And I ask myself sometimes:
The boy with dreams and love,
Where did he even go?
Is there something
He's running from?

37. Tripod

Little I ever knew,

Will meet

Such incredible souls,

Treat me

With so much love

And respect,

It's unexpected,

And eclectic

Will come across

Such a friendship,

And its beautiful aspects.
Forgotten all the reasons
The hurt, the anxiety,
And the confusion too
That connection caused
In the past.
With their coming,
And entering my life,
At the most unexpected time
Makes me feel stronger,
And I welcome both of them
With my open arms.
The journey of finding love
And learning people never ends
Coming of us, three
Have brought the Sunlight
Which we never want to lose.
We three might not know
Too much about love or feelings,
Yet we learned together
How to be tender,
And patient with those
That we care about.
Our infectious laughter,
And the warmth we emit
Nothing else can replace.
Little I knew,

With coming, us together
Everything will fall into place.

Disclaimer

"This book is a work of fiction. Any references to gender, historical events, real characters, or actual places are used fictitiously to make these stanzas. Other characters, places, and events are products of the author's imagination, and, any resemblance to actual events, places, or persons, living or dead, is entirely coincidental. There is no intention to offend anyone's sentiments."

www.ingramcontent.com/pod-product-compliance
Lightning Source LLC
Chambersburg PA
CBHW051237130726
47988CB00001B/392